Sleep-over Mouse

Written by Mary Packard
Illustrated by Kathy Wilburn

children's press ®

A Division of Scholastic Inc.
New York Toronto London Auckland Sydney
Mexico City New Delhi Hong Kong
Danbury, Connecticut

Library of Congress Cataloging-in-Publication Data

Packard, Mary.
  Sleep-over mouse / written by Mary Packard ; illustrated by Kathy
Wilburn.– 1st American ed.
      p. cm. – (My first reader)
Summary: Squeak is a little mouse who loves to sleep over at anyone's
house.
  ISBN 0-516-22936-2 (lib. bdg.)   0-516-24638-0 (pbk.)
  [1. Sleepovers–Fiction. 2. Mice–Fiction. 3. Stories in rhyme.] I.
Wilburn, Kathy, ill. II. Title. III. Series.
  PZ8.3.P125Sl 2003
  [E]–dc21
                          2003003650

Text © 1994 Nancy Hall, Inc.
Illustrations © 1994 Kathy Wilburn
Published in 2003 by Children's Press
A Division of Scholastic Inc.
All rights reserved. Published simultaneously in Canada.
Printed in the United States of America.

CHILDREN'S PRESS and associated logos are trademarks and or registered trademarks of Scholastic Library Publishin
SCHOLASTIC and associated logos are trademarks and or registered trademarks of Scholastic Inc.

1 2 3 4 5 6 7 8 9 10 R 12 11 10 09 08 07 06 05 04 03

Note to Parents and Teachers

Once a reader can recognize and identify the 34 words
used to tell this story, he or she will be able to read successfully
the entire book. These 34 words are repeated throughout the story,
so that young readers will be able to easily recognize
the words and understand their meaning.

The 34 words used in this book are:

a	is	play	there
anyone's	little	plenty	to
at	loves	share	too
can	make	sheets	toys
do	makes	sleep	treats
fun	meet	sleep-over	with
he	mouse	sleepover	you
he's	noise	Squeak	
house	over	tents	

Meet little Squeak.

He's a sleep-over mouse.

Squeak loves to sleep over

at anyone's house.

He loves to share toys.

He loves to share treats.

He loves to make noise.

He makes tents with sheets.

A sleepover is fun.

There is plenty to do!

Squeak loves to play.

He loves to sleep, too.

Can sleep-over mouse

sleep over with you?

MAIL

ABOUT THE AUTHOR

Mary Packard has been writing children's books for as long as she can remember. Packard lives in Northport, New York, with her family. Besides writing, she loves music, theater, animals, and, of course, children of all ages.

ABOUT THE ILLUSTRATOR

Kathy Wilburn grew up in Kansas City, Missouri, where she began her artistic career with Hallmark Cards after graduating from the Rhode Island School of Design. She currently lives in Portland, Oregon, where she works as a children's book illustrator.